Printed and Published in Great Britain by D. C. THOMSON & CO., LTD., 185 Fleet Street, London EC4A 2HS.
© D. C. THOMSON & CO., LTD., 1991.
ISBN 0-85116-504-4

Old Dod has been following the cart—

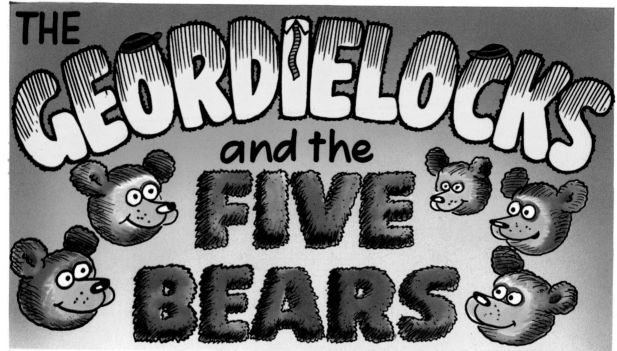

THE GEORDIELOCKS and the FIVE BEARS

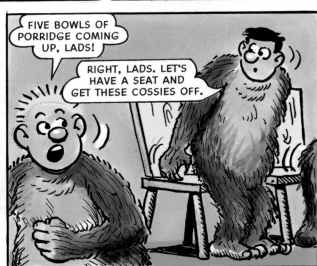

THE history of the U.S.A. is rich in tales of battles won and lost. Perhaps the most famous fight against the native red indians was fought by Lieutenant Colonel George Armstrong Custer.

In June of 1876, Yellow Hair, as the indians called Custer, led some 215 men of the 7th Cavalry against an encampment of the Sioux and Cheyenne nations, commanded by Sitting Bull and Crazy Horse.

Eager for glory, Custer refused to wait for reinforcements and charged the nations. He was hopelessly outnumbered. Crazy Horse, a master tactician, quickly had the detachment surrounded, by the Little Big Horn river. Forcing back other units of the 7th, Crazy Horse led his warriors against a stubborn Custer. Guns blazing, the unit fought to the last bullet — and last man.

Custer had found the lasting fame he sought — in the greatest defeat ever against the indians.

THE BATTLE OF THE
LITTLE

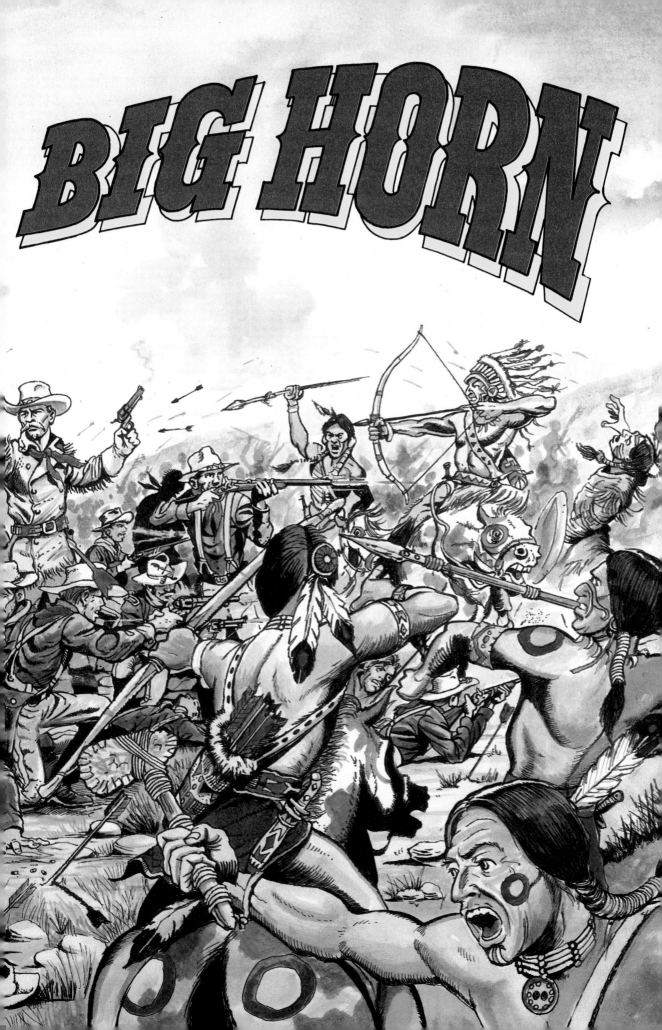

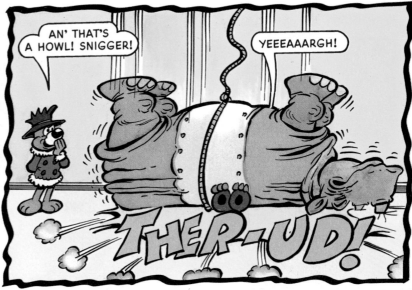

Suddenly in burst the arch party-pooper, Clarence Creep, Winker's form master!

BUT NEXT DAY . . .

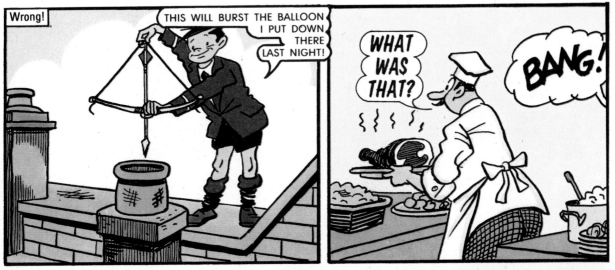

SEE! NOT A TRACE OF SOOT!

CREEPY-CRAWLIES! WHERE DID THEY COME FROM?

Winker had been collecting hundreds of insects!

UGH! BEETLES CRAWLING ABOUT EVERYWHERE!

Oh, dear! The Inspector closed the school kitchens! Winker pretended dismay.

AW, SIR! WE HAVEN'T HAD A MEAL FOR TWO DAYS.

But! Winker knew they'd be ordered to eat out!

I WON'T ALLOW YOU TO USE THE KITCHEN, SO I'M ORDERING YOU TO TAKE THESE BOYS OUT TO THE VILLAGE INN FOR A MEAL—AND AT ONCE, TOO.

COME ALONG, AND REMEMBER YOU WILL ONLY ORDER PLAIN FARE AT THE INN—NO FANCY CHRISTMAS FOOD! AND THAT GOES FOR YOU, TOO, MR CREEP!

BULLY BEEF & CHIPS

HIKING HORRORS

Several miles on . . .

PING

GURR-OWL!

GULP! QUICK, KATEY, RUN!

DON'T JUST STAND THERE LIKE A BEAR WITH A SORE HEAD! GET AFTER THEM!

GRRRR

HO-HO! THIS SAVES ME HAVING TO CARRY THEM TOO!

WELL, THEY'VE OUTRUN THE BEAR, BUT I SEE IT HAD A SWIPE AT DANNY'S PANTS!

A few miles further . . .

YUP. I'D RECOGNISE THAT 'BEAR-PATCH' ANYWHERE! I THINK I'LL HAVE A LITTLE SNACK.

BUT WHERE WOULD BANANAMAN HAVE HIS SECRET HIDE-OUT? I'M STUMPED!

BANANA WAREHOUSE

WHAT A BUSY DAY I'VE HAD! SEVENTEEN ROBBERIES WITH ONLY ONE TEA-BREAK. I'LL HAVE A RELAXING READ, AND WAIT FOR LOW DOWN SCOUNDREL MAN TO FIND ME!

NO NOTICES ON THIS WALL

OKAY, BANANAMAN — YOUR STOLEN GOODS AND YOUR SUPER-THIEVING GEAR, OR YOUR LIFE!

HOW DID YOU FIND MY SECRET HIDE-OUT, LOW DOWN SCOUNDREL MAN?

BANANA WAREHOUSE

CALL IT A WILD GUESS!

I'VE HAD A THOUGHT, CHIEF! IT'S SO OBVIOUS — BANANAMAN MUST BE HIDING OUT IN AN ORANGES WAREHOUSE!

YOU MAY BE ONTO SOMETHING THERE . . .

WELL! WHILE YOU LOT WERE READING THAT AWFUL JOKE ROUTINE, SCOUNDREL MAN AND I HAD THE MOST SPECTACULAR FIGHT!

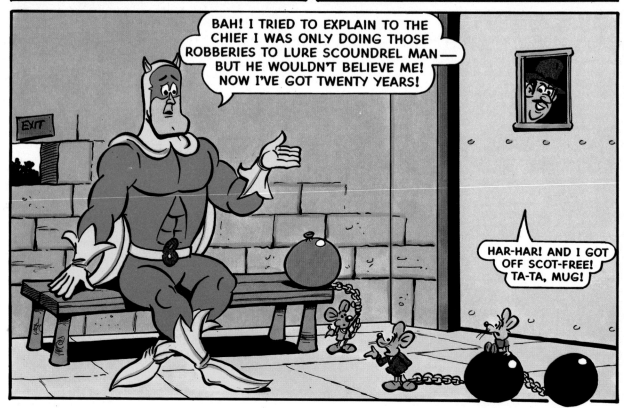

REMEMBER THE

IN the 1830's the territory of Texas actually belonged to Mexico, though many of its settlers were Americans.

The Mexican President, Santa Anna, wanted rid of these Americans and set out with an army to clear them out. He marched into Texas expecting little resistance. His own force was well armed and disciplined, while the hastily formed Texas Volunteers had few supplies and little training.

To buy his army valuable time, Lieutenant Colonel William Travis made a stand at a little mission called the Alamo, outside San Antonio. There he was joined by the legendary Jim Bowie and Davy Crockett with his Tennessee sharpshooters.

A force of 183 men against 4000 Mexican regulars!

The battle didn't last long. In ninety minutes of fierce hand to hand combat every single defender was killed — but they took over 800 Mexican troops with them!

Santa Anna hadn't been delayed for long, but the defeat of their brave band put heart into every Texan. From that day the Mexicans would hear the war cry "Remember The Alamo!" at every battle. Santa Anna was driven from Texas for ever, defeated by his own victory!

Americans will always remember The Alamo.

MASKED BRAWL!

STARRING

MUTT and MOGGY

Mutt and Moggy, your canine and feline friends were becoming sick of the sight of each other, so . . .

THE INCREDIBLE T-SHIRT

IN
THE SEARCH FOR SADIE SIDEBOTTOM

TEN-YEAR-OLD 'Piggy' Sidebottom, who made oinking noises while he ate, lived with his Mum in a tumbledown cottage on the outskirts of the tumbledown village of Little Happening. They were so poor that the mice handed back the cheese out of the traps! One day a few weeks before Christmas . . .

Aah! My mother came from Auchtermuchty and her clootie dumplings were Scotland's finest.

Oink — hey — wait an oinking minute . . . that's a Dandy T-shirt . . . and it's in better oinking nick than the rags I'm wearing.

SLURP!

Footnote →

A clootie dumpling is considered a rare treat in Scotland . . . and it's easier caught than haggis!

Later—

Hi, Mum. I washed it in a puddle at the front door — our water's been cut off.

You look right smart, Piggy — but what can I wrap the dumpling in?

WHOOSH!
If there's one thing I like better than Smarties — it's a nice cup of tea.
Must say — I oink — agree with you! Oink! Oink!
Come on, follow me — this yarn's beginning to drag a bit.
Huh! Now he's a literary critic!
The trail finally ended at a post box — right outside Piggy's front door!
Are you in there, Sadie?
Yes! And it's taken you 42 years to find me!

TRISTAN

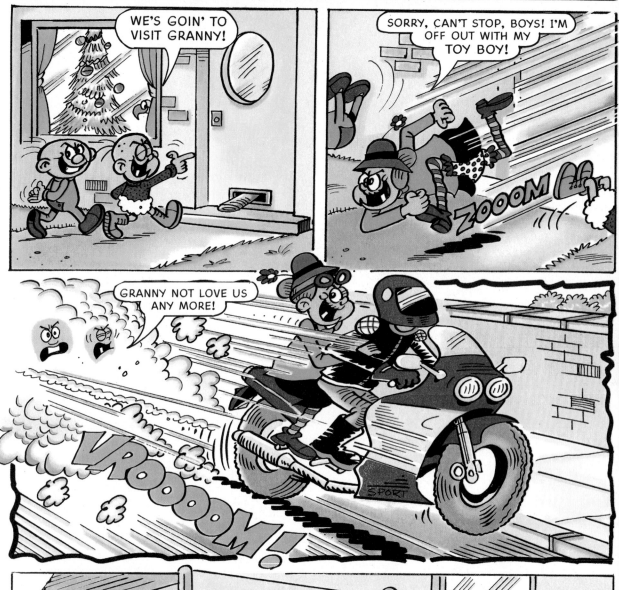

Desperate DAN

PRESENT DAY   VICTORIAN   18th CENTURY   A LONG TIME AGO   CAVE JOCK

the JOCKS and THE GEORDIES
WORLD HISTORY

CAVE GEORDIE   ROMAN   MEDIAEVAL   EDWARDIAN   PRESENT DAY

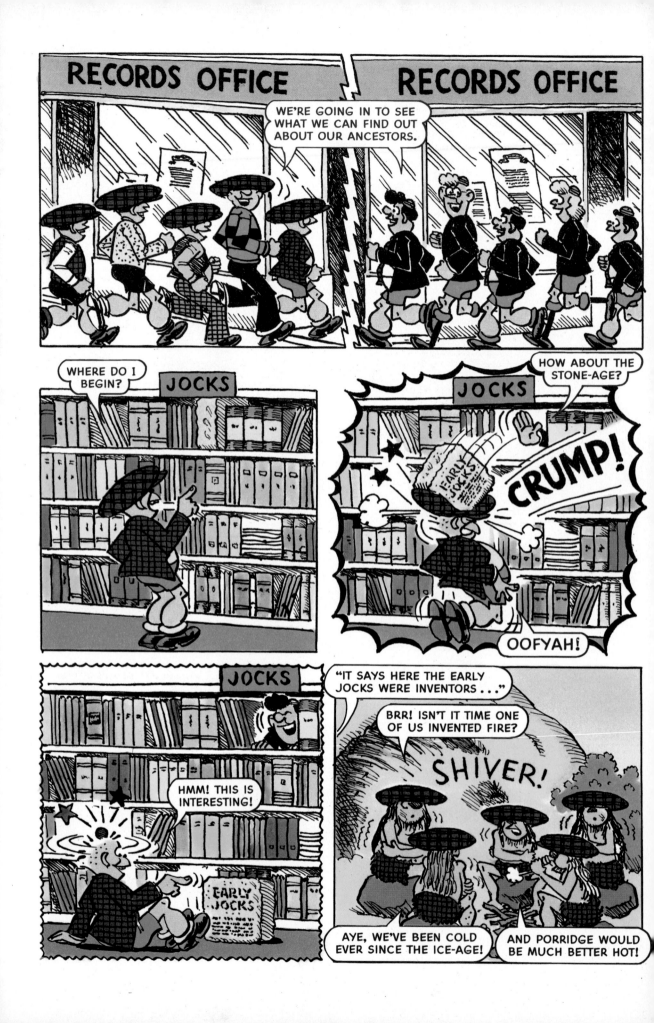